Under My Feet

Rabbits

Patricia Whitehouse

Heinemann Library
Chicago, Illinois

Customer Service 888-454-2279
Visit our website at www.heinemannlibrary.com

Designed by Sue Emerson, Heinemann Library; Page layout by Que-Net Media™
Printed and bound in the United States by Lake Book Manufacturing, Inc.
Photo research by Bill Broyles

08 07 06 05 04
10 9 8 7 6 5 4 3 2 1

Library of Congress Cataloging-in-Publication Data
Whitehouse, Patricia, 1958-
  Rabbits / Patricia Whitehouse.
      v. cm. – (Under my feet)
Contents: Do rabbits live here? – What are rabbits? – What do rabbits look like? – Where do rabbits live? – What do rabbit homes look like? – How do rabbits find their way underground? – How do rabbits make their homes? – What is special about rabbit homes? – When do rabbits come out from underground? – Rabbit home map.
  ISBN 1-4034-4321-1 (HC), 1-4034-4330-0 (Pbk.)
  1. Rabbits–Juvenile literature. [1. Rabbits.] I. Title.
  QL737.L32W465 2003
  599.32–dc21

2003000052

Acknowledgments
The author and publishers are grateful to the following for permission to reproduce copyright material:
p. 4 Photodisc Green; pp. 5, 9 Ian Beames/Ardea London Ltd.; p. 6 Photo Researchers, Inc.; p. 7 Michael Leach/NHPA; pp. 8, 10, 12, 14, 16, 17 Oxford Scientific Films; p. 11 Ernest Janes/Photo Researchers, Inc.; p. 13 David C. Reniz/Bruce Coleman Inc.; pp. 15, 19 Maurice Tibbles/SAL/Oxford Scientific Films; p. 18 Stone/Getty Images; p. 20 Des & Jen Barlett/SAL/Oxford Scientific Films.; p. 21 Simon King/Naturepl.com; p. 23 (column 1, T-B) Maurice Tibbles/SAL/Oxford Scientific Films, Ernest Janes/Photo Researchers, Inc., Photo Researchers, Inc.; (column 2, T-B) Oxford Scientific Films, Oxford Scientific Films, David C. Reniz/Bruce Coleman Inc.; back cover Oxford Scientific Films

Illustration on page 22 by Will Hobbs
Cover photograph by Ian Beames/Ardea London Ltd.

Every effort has been made to contact copyright holders of any material reproduced in this book. Any omissions will be rectified in subsequent printings if notice is given to the publisher.

Special thanks to our advisory panel for their help in the preparation of this book:

Alice Bethke, Library Consultant
Palo Alto, CA

Eileen Day, Preschool Teacher
Chicago, IL

Kathleen Gilbert,
Second Grade Teacher
Round Rock, TX

Sandra Gilbert,
Library Media Specialist
Fiest Elementary School
Houston, TX

Jan Gobeille,
Kindergarten Teacher
Garfield Elementary
Oakland, CA

Angela Leeper,
Educational Consultant
Wake Forest, NC

Special thanks to Mark Rosenthal, Abra Prentice Wilkin Curator of Large Mammals at Chicago's Lincoln Park Zoo, for his help in the preparation of this book.

Some words are shown in bold, **like this.**
You can find them in the picture glossary on page 23.

Contents

Do Rabbits Live Here?

When you walk outside, you might not see a rabbit.

But you might be walking over one.

Some rabbits live under your feet.

Their homes are underground.

What Are Rabbits?

Rabbits are **mammals.**

Mammals have hair or fur on their bodies.

Mammals make milk for their babies.

These are new baby rabbits.

What Do Rabbits Look Like?

ear   tail   leg

Rabbits have long ears and long back legs.

Their tails are small and fluffy.

Most rabbits are brown or gray.

Rabbits are about the size of a cat.

Where Do Rabbits Live?

Most rabbits do not live with people.

Some live alone underground.

Other rabbits live together in a group called a **colony**.

Rabbits can live in warm or cold places.

What Do Rabbit Homes Look Like?

Rabbits live in **burrows.**

Burrows have **tunnels** and a **nest.**

Very big burrows are called **warrens.**

Many rabbits live in a warren.

How Do They Find Their Way?

Rabbits use their big ears to hear.

They can hear sounds outside their **burrow**.

Rabbits use their noses to smell.

A mother rabbit can find her babies by their smell.

How Do Rabbits Make Their Homes?

Rabbits dig dirt with their paws.

They push the dirt out.

Rabbits put grass in their **nests.**

Grass keeps baby rabbits warm and dry.

What Is Special About Their Homes?

Most **burrows** have many ways to get in.

This helps rabbits get away from danger quickly.

A mother rabbit keeps her babies safe.

When she leaves the **nest,** she closes the hole to the nest.

When Do Rabbits Come Out from Underground?

Rabbits come out from underground to eat.

They eat in the morning and late afternoon.

Rabbits may leave their **burrows** if there is danger.

Most burrows have many ways to get out.

Rabbit Home Map

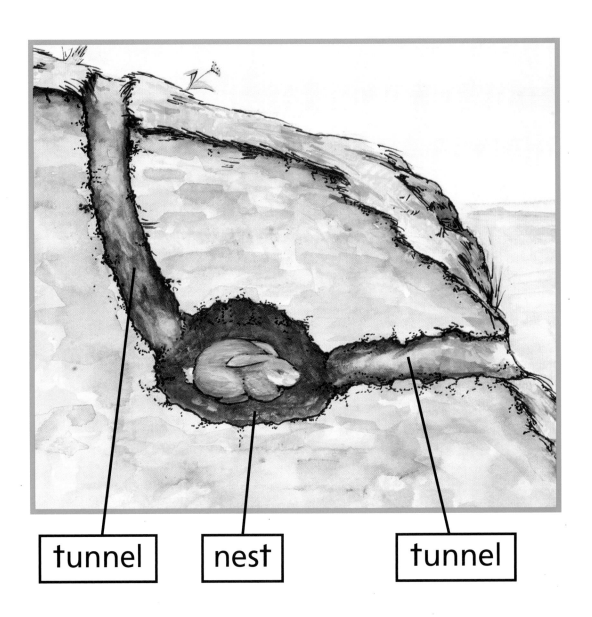

tunnel   nest   tunnel

Picture Glossary

burrow
pages 12, 13, 14,
   18, 21

nest
pages 12, 17,
   19, 22

colony
page 11

tunnel
pages 12, 22

mammal
pages 6, 7

warren
page 13

Note to Parents and Teachers

Reading for information is an important part of a child's literacy development. Learning begins with a question about something. Help children think of themselves as investigators and researchers by encouraging their questions about the world around them. Each chapter in this book begins with a question. Read the question together. Look at the pictures. Talk about what you think the answer might be. Then read the text to find out if your predictions were correct. Think of other questions you could ask about the topic, and discuss where you might find the answers. Assist children in using the picture glossary and the index to practice new vocabulary and research skills.

 CAUTION: Remind children that it is not a good idea to handle wild animals or insects. Children should wash their hands with soap and water after they touch any animal.

Index